THE BACCHAE

OF EURIPIDES

Translated by GILBERT MURRAY

The Bacchae
By Euripides
Translated by Gilbert Murray

Print ISBN 13: 978-1-4209-6183-6
eBook ISBN 13: 978-1-4209-6184-3

Cover Image: a detail of a Roman fresco. Pentheus being torn by maenads. House of Vettii. Pompeii. Italy. / Tarker / Bridgeman Images.

Please visit *www.digireads.com*

CONTENTS

INTRODUCTORY NOTE 5

DRAMATIS PERSONAE 6

THE BACCHAE 7

INTRODUCTORY NOTE

Euripides, the youngest of the trio of great Greek tragedians was born at Salamis in 480 B.C., on the day when the Greeks won their momentous naval victory there over the fleet of the Persians. The precise social status of his parents is not clear but he received a good education, was early distinguished as an athlete, and showed talent in painting and oratory. He was a fellow student of Pericles, and his dramas show the influence of the philosophical ideas of Anaxagoras and of Socrates, with whom he was personally intimate. Like Socrates, he was accused of impiety, and this, along with domestic infelicity, has been supposed to afford a motive for his withdrawal from Athens, first to Magnesia and later to the court of Archelaues in Macedonia where he died in 406 B.C.

The first tragedy of Euripides was produced when he was about twenty-five, and he was several times a victor in the tragic contests. In spite of the antagonisms which he aroused and the criticisms which were hurled upon him in, for example, the comedies of Aristophanes, he attained a very great popularity; and Plutarch tells that those Athenians who were taken captive in the disastrous Sicilian expedition of 413 B.C. were offered freedom by their captors if they could recite from the works of Euripides. Of the hundred and twenty dramas ascribed to Euripides, there have come down to us complete eighteen tragedies and one satyric drama, "Cyclops," beside numerous fragments.

The works of Euripides are generally regarded as showing the beginning of the decline of Greek tragedy. The idea of Fate hitherto dominant in the plays of his predecessors, tends to be degraded by him into mere chance; the characters lose much of their ideal quality; and even gods and heroes are represented as moved by the petty motives of ordinary humanity. The chorus is often quite detached from the action; the poetry is florid; and the action is frequently tinged with sensationalism. In spite of all this, Euripides remains a great poet; and his picturesqueness and tendencies to what are now called realism and romanticism, while marking his inferiority to the chaste classicism of Sophocles, bring him more easily within the sympathetic interest of the modern reader.

DRAMATIS PERSONAE

DIONYSUS, THE GOD; *son of Zeus and of the Theban princess Semelê.*
CADMUS, *formerly King of Thebes, father of Semelê.*
PENTHEUS, *King of Thebes, grandson of Cadmus.*
AGÂVÊ, *daughter of Cadmus, mother of Pentheus.*
TEIRESIAS, *an aged Theban prophet.*
A SOLDIER OF PENTHEUS' GUARD.
TWO MESSENGERS.
A CHORUS OF INSPIRED DAMSELS, *following Dionysus from the East.*

"The play was first produced after the death of Euripides by his son who bore the same name, together with the 'Iphigenia in Aulis' and the 'Alcmaeon,' probably in the year 405 B.C."

THE BACCHAE

[*The background represents the front of the Castle of* PENTHEUS,
*King of Thebes. At one side is visible the sacred Tomb of
Semelê, a little enclosure overgrown with wild vines, with a
cleft in the rocky floor of it from which there issues at times
steam or smoke. The God* DIONYSUS *is discovered alone.*]

DIONYSUS. Behold, God's Son is come unto this land
Of heaven's hot splendour lit to life, when she
Of Thebes, even I, Dionysus, whom the brand
Who bore me, Cadmus' daughter Semelê,
Died here. So, changed in shape from God to man,
I walk again by Dircê's streams and scan
Ismenus' shore. There by the castle side
I see her place, the Tomb of the Lightning's Bride,
The wreck of smouldering chambers, and the great
Faint wreaths of fire undying—as the hate
Dies not, that Hera held for Semelê.
Aye, Cadmus hath done well; in purity
He keeps this place apart, inviolate,
His daughter's sanctuary; and I have set
My green and clustered vines to robe it round
Far now behind me lies the golden ground
Of Lydian and of Phrygian; far away
The wide hot plains where Persian sunbeams play,
The Bactrian war-holds, and the storm-oppressed
Clime of the Mede, and Araby the Blest,
And Asia all, that by the salt sea lies[1]
In proud embattled cities, motley-wise
Of Hellene and Barbarian interwrought;
And now I come to Hellas—having taught
All the world else my dances and my rite
Of mysteries, to show me in men's sight
Manifest God.
                    And first of Helene lands
I cry this Thebes to waken; set her hands
To clasp my wand, mine ivied javelin,
And round her shoulders hang my wild fawn-skin.
For they have scorned me whom it least beseemed,
Semelê's sisters; mocked by birth, nor deemed
That Dionysus sprang from Dian seed.[2]

---

[1] *i.e.* the coasts of Asia Minor inhabited by Greeks, Ionia, Aeolis, and Doris.

My mother sinned, said they; and in her need,
With Cadmus plotting, cloaked her human shame
With the dread name of Zeus; for that the flame
From heaven consumed her, seeing she lied to God.
Thus must they vaunt; and therefore hath my rod
On them first fallen, and stung them forth wild-eyed
From empty chambers; the bare mountain side
Is made their home, and all their hearts are flame.
Yea, I have bound upon the necks of them
The harness of my rites. And with them all
The seed of womankind from hut and hall
Of Thebes, hath this my magic goaded out.
And there, with the old King's daughters, in a rout
Confused, they make their dwelling-place between
The roofless rocks and shadowy pine trees green.
Thus shall this Thebes, how sore soe'er it smart,
Learn and forget not, till she crave her part
In mine adoring; thus must I speak clear
To save my mother's fame, and crown me here,
As true God, born by Semelê to Zeus.

Now Cadmus yieldeth up his throne and use
Of royal honour to his daughter's son
Pentheus; who on my body hath begun
A war with God. He thrusteth me away
From due drink-offering, and, when men pray,
My name entreats not. Therefore on his own
Head and his people's shall my power be shown.
Then to another land, when all things here
Are well, must I fare onward, making clear
My godhead's might. But should this Theban town
Essay with wrath and battle to drag down[3]
My maids, lo, in their path myself shall be,
And maniac armies battled after me!
For this I veil my godhead with the wan
Form of the things that die, and walk as Man.

O Brood of Tmolus o'er the wide world flown,
O Lydian band, my chosen and mine own,
Damsels uplifted o'er the orient deep

---

[2] Dian = belonging to Zeus. The name Dionysus seemed to be derived from
Διός, the genitive of "Zeus."
[3] This suggestion of a possibility which is never realised or approached is
perhaps a mark of the unrevised condition of the play. The same may be said of the
repetitions in the Prologue.

To wander where I wander, and to sleep
Where I sleep; up, and wake the old sweet sound,
The clang that I and mystic Rhea found,
The Timbrel of the Mountain! Gather all
Thebes to your song round Pentheus' royal hall.
I seek my new-made worshippers, to guide
Their dances up Kithaeron's pine clad side.

[*As he departs, there comes stealing in from the left a band of
fifteen Eastern Women, the light of the sunrise streaming upon
their long white robes and ivy-bound hair. They wear fawn-
skins over the robes, and carry some of them timbrels, some
pipes and other instruments. Many bear the thyrsus, or sacred
Wand, made of reed ringed with ivy. They enter stealthily till
they see that the place is empty, and then begin their mystic
song of worship.*]

CHORUS.

A MAIDEN. From Asia, from the dayspring that uprises
    To Bromios ever glorying we came.
  We laboured for our Lord in many guises;
  We toiled, but the toil is as the prize is;
    Thou Mystery, we hail thee by thy name!
ANOTHER. Who lingers in the road? Who espies us?
    He shall hide him in his house nor be bold.
  Let the heart keep silence that defies us;
  For I sing this day to Dionysus
    The song that is appointed from of old.
ALL THE MAIDENS. Oh, blessed he in all wise,
    Who hath drunk the Living Fountain,
      Whose life no folly staineth,
        And his soul is near to God;
  Whose sins are lifted, pall-wise,
    As he worships on the Mountain,
      And where Cybelê ordaineth,
        Our Mother, he has trod:

His head with ivy laden
  And his thyrsus tossing high,
    For our God he lifts his cry;
"Up, O Bacchae, wife and maiden,
    Come, O ye Bacchae, come;
Oh, bring the Joy-bestower,
God-seed of God the Sower,

Bring Bromios in his power
    From Phrygia's mountain dome;
To street and town and tower,
    Oh, bring ye Bromios home."

Whom erst in anguish lying
    For an unborn life's desire,
      As a dead thing in the Thunder
      His mother cast to earth;
For her heart was dying, dying,
    In the white heart of the fire;
      Till Zeus, the Lord of Wonder,
      Devised new lairs of birth;

Yea, his own flesh tore to hide him,
    And with clasps of bitter gold
    Did a secret son enfold,
    And the Queen knew not beside him;
      Till the perfect hour was there;
    Then a horned God was found,
    And a God of serpents crowned;
    And for that are serpents wound
      In the wands his maidens bear,
    And the songs of serpents sound
      In the mazes of their hair.

SOME MAIDENS. All hail, O Thebes, thou nurse of Semelê!
    With Semelê's wild ivy crown thy towers;
  Oh, burst in bloom of wreathing bryony,
      Berries and leaves and flowers;
    Uplift the dark divine wand,
    The oak-wand and the pine-wand,
And don thy fawn-skin, fringed in purity
    With fleecy white, like ours.

Oh, cleanse thee in the wands' waving pride!
    Yea, all men shall dance with us and pray,
When Bromios his companies shall guide
    Hillward, ever hillward, where they stay,
      The flock of the Believing,
      The maids from loom and weaving
By the magic of his breath borne away.

OTHERS. Hail thou, O Nurse of Zeus, O Caverned Haunt
    Where fierce arms clanged to guard God's cradle rare,
For thee of old crested Corybant
    First woke in Cretan air

The wild orb of our orgies,
Our Timbrel; and thy gorges
Rang with this strain; and blended Phrygian chant
And sweet keen pipes were there.

But the Timbrel, the Timbrel was another's,
And away to Mother Rhea it must wend;
And to our holy singing from the Mother's
The mad Satyrs carried it, to blend
In the dancing and the cheer
Of our third and perfect Year;
And it serves Dionysus in the end!

A MAIDEN. O glad, glad on the mountains
To swoon in the race outworn,
When the holy fawn-skin clings,
And all else sweeps away,
To the joy of the red quick fountains,
The blood of the hill-goat torn,
The glory of wild-beast ravenings,
Where the hill-tops catch the day;
To the Phrygian, Lydian, mountains!
'Tis Bromios leads the way.

ANOTHER MAIDEN. Then streams the earth with milk, yea, streams
With wine and nectar of the bee,
And through the air dim perfume steams
Of Syrian frankincense; and He,
Our leader, from his thyrsus spray
A torchlight tosses high and higher,
A torchlight like a beacon-fire,
To waken all that faint and stray;
And sets them leaping as he sings,
His tresses rippling to the sky,
And deep beneath the Maenad cry
His proud voice rings:
"Come, O ye Bacchae, come!"

ALL THE MAIDENS. Hither, O fragrant of Tmolus the Golden,
Come with the voice of timbrel and drum;
Let the cry of your joyance uplift and embolden
The God of the joy-cry; O Bacchanals, come!
With pealing of pipes and with Phrygian clamour,
On, where the vision of holiness thrills,
And the music climbs and the maddening glamour,
With the wild White Maids, to the hills, to the hills!
Oh, then, like a colt as he runs by a river,
A colt by his dam, when the heart of him sings,

With the keen limbs drawn and the fleet foot a-quiver,
    Away the Bacchanal springs![4]

[Enter TEIRESIAS. *He is an old man and blind, leaning upon a staff
and moving with slow stateliness, though wearing the Ivy and
the Bacchic fawn-skin.]*

TEIRESIAS. Ho, there, who keeps the gate?—Go, summon me
  Cadmus, Agênor's son, who crossed the sea
  From Sidon and upreared this Theban hold.
  Go, whosoe'er thou art. See he be told
  Teiresias seeketh him. Himself will gauge
  Mine errand, and the compact, age with age,
  I vowed with him, grey hair with snow-white hair,
  To deck the new God's thyrsus, and to wear
  His fawn-skin, and with ivy crown our brows.

[Enter CADMUS *from the Castle. He is even older than* TEIRESIAS,
and wears the same attire.]

CADMUS. True friend! I knew that voice of thine, that flows
  Like mellow wisdom from a fountain wise.
  And, lo, I come prepared, in all the guise
  And harness of this God. Are we not told
  His is the soul of that dead life of old
  That sprang from mine own daughter? Surely then
  Must thou and I with all the strength of men
  Exalt him.
           Where then shall I stand, where tread
  The dance and toss this bowed and hoary head?
  O friend, in thee is wisdom; guide my grey
  And eld-worn steps, eld-worn Teiresias.—Nay;
  I am not weak.

*[At the first movement of worship his manner begins to change; a
mysterious strength and exaltation enter into him.]*

---

[4] This first song of the Chorus covers a great deal of Bacchic doctrine and
myth. The first strophe, "Oh blessed he in all wise," &c, describes the bliss of
Bacchic purity; the antistrophe gives the two births of Dionysus, from Semele and
from the body of Zeus, mentioning his mystic epiphanies as Bull and as Serpent.
The next strophe is an appeal to Thebes, the birthplace or "nurse" of the God's
mother, Semele; the antistrophe, an appeal to the cavern in Crete, the birthplace of
Zeus, the God's father, and the original home of the mystic Timbrel. The Epode, or
closing song, is full, not of doctrine, but of the pure poetry of the worship.

> Surely this arm could smite
The wild earth with its thyrsus, day and night,
And faint not! Sweetly and forgetfully
The dim years fall from off me!

TEIRESIAS. As with thee,
> With me 'tis likewise. Light am I and young,
And will essay the dancing and the song.

CADMUS. Quick, then, our chariots to the mountain road.
TEIRESIAS. Nay; to take steeds were to mistrust the God.
CADMUS. So be it. Mine old arms shall guide thee there.
TEIRESIAS. The God himself shall guide! Have thou no care.
CADMUS. And in all Thebes shall no man dance but we?
TEIRESIAS. Aye, Thebes is blinded. Thou and I can see.
CADMUS. 'Tis weary waiting; hold my hand, friend; so.
TEIRESIAS. Lo, there is mine. So linked let us go.
CADMUS. Shall things of dust the Gods' dark ways despise?
TEIRESIAS. Or prove our wit on Heaven's high mysteries?

> Not thou and I! That heritage sublime
Our sires have left us, wisdom old as time,
No word of man, how deep soe'er his thought
And won of subtlest toil, may bring to naught.

> Aye, men will rail that I forgot my years,
To dance and wreath with ivy these white hairs;
What recks it? Seeing the God no line hath told
To mark what man shall dance, or young or old;
But craves his honours from mortality
All, no man marked apart; and great shall be!

CADMUS. [*after looking away toward the Mountain.*] Teiresias, since
> this light thou canst not read,
I must be seer for thee. Here comes in speed
Pentheus, Echîon's son, whom I have raised
To rule my people in my stead.—Amazed
He seems. Stand close, and mark what we shall hear.

[*The two stand back, partially concealed, while there enters in hot
haste* PENTHEUS, *followed by a bodyguard. He is speaking to
the* SOLDIER *in command.*]

PENTHEUS. Scarce had I crossed our borders, when mine ear[5]
    Was caught by this strange rumour, that our own
    Wives, our own sisters, from their hearths are flown
    To wild and secret rites; and cluster there
    High on the shadowy hills, with dance and prayer
    To adore this new-made God, this Dionyse,
    Whate'er he be!—And in their companies
    Deep wine-jars stand, and ever and anon
    Away into the loneliness now one
    Steals forth, and now a second, maid or dame
    Where love lies waiting, not of God! The flame
    They say, of Bacchios wraps them. Bacchios! Nay,
    'Tis more to Aphrodite that they pray.
      Howbeit, all that I have found, my men
    Hold bound and shackled in our dungeon den;
    The rest, I will go hunt them! Aye, and snare
    My birds with nets of iron, to quell their prayer
    And mountain song and rites of rascaldom!
      They tell me, too, there is a stranger come,
    A man of charm and spell, from Lydian seas,
    A head all gold and cloudy fragrancies,
    A wine-red cheek, and eyes that hold the light
    Of the very Cyprian. Day and livelong night
    He haunts amid the damsels, o'er each lip
    Dangling his cup of joyance! Let me grip
    Him once, but once, within these walls, right swift
    That wand shall cease its music, and that drift
    Of tossing curls lie still—when my rude sword
    Falls between neck and trunk! 'Tis all his word,
    This tale of Dionysus; how that same
    Babe that was blasted by the lightning flame
    With his dead mother, for that mother's lie,
    Was reconceived, born perfect from the thigh
    Of Zeus, and now is God! What call ye these?
    Dreams? Gibes of the unknown wanderer? Blasphemies
    That crave the very gibbet?
                    Stay! God wot,
    Here is another marvel! See I not

---

    [5] Pentheus, though his case against the new worship is so good, and he might so easily have been made into a fine martyr, like Hippolytus, is left harsh and unpleasant, and very close in type to the ordinary "tyrant" of Greek tragedy (cf. p. 46). It is also noteworthy, I think, that he is, as it were, out of tone with the other characters. He belongs to a different atmosphere, like, to take a recent instance, Golaud in *Pelléas et Mélisande*.

In motley fawn-skins robed the vision-seer
Teiresias? And my mother's father here—
O depth of scorn!—adoring with the wand
Of Bacchios?—Father!—Nay, mine eyes are fond;
It is not your white heads so fancy-flown!
It cannot be! Cast off that ivy crown,
O mine own mother's sire! Set free that hand
That cowers about its staff.
               'Tis thou hast planned
This work, Teiresias! 'Tis thou must set
Another altar and another yet
Amongst us, watch new birds, and win more hire
Of gold, interpreting new signs of fire!
But for thy silver hairs, I tell thee true,
Thou now wert sitting chained amid thy crew
Of raving damsels, for this evil dream
Thou hast brought us, of new Gods! When once the gleam
Of grapes hath lit a Woman's Festival,
In all their prayers is no more health at all!
LEADER OF THE CHORUS. [*the words are not heard by* PENTHEUS.]
    Injurious King, hast thou no fear of God,[6]
    Nor Cadmus, sower of the Giants' Sod,[7]
    Life-spring to great Echîon and to thee?
TEIRESIAS. Good words my son, come easily, when he
    That speaks is wise, and speaks but for the right.
Else come they never! Swift are thine, and bright
As though with thought, yet have no thought at all
    Lo, this new God, whom thou dost flout withal,
I cannot speak the greatness wherewith He
In Hellas shall be great! Two spirits there be,
Young Prince, that in man's world are first of worth.
Dêmêtêr one is named; she is the Earth—
Call her which name thou will!—who feeds man's frame
With sustenance of things dry. And that which came
Her work to perfect, second, is the Power
From Semelê born. He found the liquid show
Hid in the grape. He rests man's spirit dim
From grieving, when the vine exalteth him.
He giveth sleep to sink the fretful day

---

[6] It is a mark of a certain yielding to stage convention in Euripides' later style, that he allows the Chorus Leader to make remarks which are not "asides," but are yet not heard or noticed by anybody.

[7] Cadmus, by divine guidance, slew a dragon and sowed the teeth of it like seed in the "Field of Ares." From the teeth rose a harvest of Earth-born, or "Giant" warriors, of whom Echîon was one.

In cool forgetting. Is there any way
With man's sore heart, save only to forget?
    Yea, being God, the blood of him is set
Before the Gods in sacrifice, that we
For his sake may be blest.—And so, to thee,
That fable shames him, how this God was knit
Into God's flesh? Nay, learn the truth of it
Cleared from the false.[8]—When from that deadly light
Zeus saved the babe, and up to Olympus' height
Raised him, and Hera's wrath would cast him thence
Then Zeus devised him a divine defence.
A fragment of the world-encircling fire[9]
He rent apart, and wrought to his desire
Of shape and hue, in the image of the child,
And gave to Hera's rage. And so, beguiled
By change and passing time, this tale was born,
How the babe-god was hidden in the torn
Flesh of his sire. He hath no shame thereby.
    A prophet is he likewise. Prophecy
Cleaves to all frenzy, but beyond all else
To frenzy of prayer. Then in us verily dwells
The God himself, and speaks the thing to be.
Yea, and of Ares' realm a part hath he.
When mortal armies, mailed and arrayed,
Have in strange fear, or ever blade met blade,
Fled maddened, 'tis this God hath palsied them.
Aye, over Delphi's rock-built diadem
Thou yet shalt see him leaping with his train
Of fire across the twin-peaked mountain-plain,
Flaming the darkness with his mystic wand,
And great in Hellas.—List and understand,
King Pentheus! Dream not thou that force is power;
Nor, if thou hast a thought, and that thought sour
And sick, oh, dream not thought is wisdom!—Up,
Receive this God to Thebes; pour forth the cup
Of sacrifice, and pray, and wreathe thy brow.
    Thou fearest for the damsels? Think thee now;
How toucheth this the part of Dionyse
To hold maids pure perforce? In them it lies,

---

[8] This timid essay in rationalism reminds one of similar efforts in Pindar (e.g. *Ol.* i.). It is the product of a religious and unspeculative mind, not feeling difficulties itself, but troubled by other people's questions and objections. (See above on Teiresias.)

[9] This fire, or ether, was the ordinary material of which phantoms or apparitions were made.

And their own hearts; and in the wildest rite
Cometh no stain to her whose heart is white.
   Nay, mark me! Thou hast thy joy, when the Gate
Stands thronged, and Pentheus' name is lifted great
And high by Thebes in clamour; shall not He
Rejoice in his due meed of majesty?
   Howbeit, this Cadmus whom thou scorn'st and I
Will wear His crown, and tread His dances! Aye,
Our hairs are white, yet shall that dance be trod!
I will not lift mine arm to war with God
For thee nor all thy words. Madness most fell
Is on thee, madness wrought by some dread spell,
But not by spell nor leechcraft to be cured!

CHORUS. Grey prophet, worthy of Phoebus is thy word,
   And wise in honouring Bromios, our great God.

CADMUS. My son, right well Teiresias points thy road.
   Oh, make thine habitation here with us,
Not lonely, against men's uses. Hazardous
Is this quick bird-like beating of thy thought
Where no thought dwells.—Grant that this God be naught,
Yet let that Naught be Somewhat in thy mouth;
Lie boldly, and say He is! So north and south
Shall marvel, how there sprang a thing divine
From Semelê's flesh, and honour all our line.

[*Drawing nearer to* PENTHEUS.]

   Is there not blood before thine eyes even now?
Our lost Actaeon's blood, whom long ago
His own red hounds through yonder forest dim
Tore unto death, because he vaunted him
Against most holy Artemis? Oh, beware
And let me wreathe thy temples. Make thy prayer
With us, and walk thee humbly in God's sight.

[*He makes as if to set the wreath on* PENTHEUS *head.*]

PENTHEUS. Down with that hand! Aroint thee to thy rite
   Nor smear on me thy foul contagion!

[*Turning upon* TEIRESIAS.]

This
Thy folly's head and prompter shall not miss
The justice that he needs!—Go, half my guard
Forth to the rock-seat where he dwells in ward
O'er birds and wonders; rend the stone with crown
And trident; make one wreck of high and low
And toss his bands to all the winds of air!
    Ha, have I found the way to sting thee, there?
The rest, forth through the town! And seek amain
This girl-faced stranger, that hath wrought such bane
To all Thebes, preying on our maids and wives
Seek till ye find; and lead him here in gyves,
Till he be judged and stoned and weep in blood
The day he troubled Pentheus with his God!

[*The guards set forth in two bodies;* PENTHEUS *goes into the*
    Castle.]

TEIRESIAS. Hard heart, how little dost thou know what seed
    Thou sowest! Blind before, and now indeed
    Most mad!—Come, Cadmus, let us go our way,
    And pray for this our persecutor, pray
    For this poor city, that the righteous God
    Move not in anger.—Take thine ivy rod
    And help my steps, as I help thine. 'Twere ill,
    If two old men should fall by the roadway. Still,
    Come what come may, our service shall be done
    To Bacchios, the All-Father's mystic son
        O Pentheus, named of sorrow! Shall he claim
    From all thy house fulfilment of his name,
    Old Cadmus?—Nay, I speak not from mine art,
    But as I see—blind words and a blind heart![10][11]

---

[10] Teiresias seems to be not a spokesman of the poet's own views—far from it—but a type of the more cultured sort of Dionysiac priest, not very enlightened, but ready to abate some of the extreme dogmas of his creed if he may keep the rest. Cadmus, quite a different character, takes a very human and earthly point of view: the God is probably a true God; but even if he is false, there is no great harm done, and the worship will bring renown to Thebes and the royal family. It is noteworthy how full of pity Cadmus is—the sympathetic kindliness of the sons of this world as contrasted with the pitilessness of gods and their devotees. See especially the last scenes of the play. Even his final outburst of despair at not dying like other men (p. 80), shows the same sympathetic humanity.

[11] These three speeches are very clearly contrasted. Cadmus, thoroughly human, thinking of sympathy and expediency, and vividly remembering the fate of

[*The two Old Men go off towards the Mountain.*]

CHORUS

SOME MAIDENS. Thou Immaculate on high;
  Thou Recording Purity;[12]
  Thou that stoopest, Golden Wing,
  Earthward, manward, pitying,
  Hearest thou this angry King?
  Hearest thou the rage and scorn
    'Gainst the Lord of Many Voices,
  Him of mortal mother born,
    Him in whom man's heart rejoices,
  Girt with garlands and with glee,
  First in Heaven's sovranty?
    For his kingdom, it is there,
    In the dancing and the prayer,
  In the music and the laughter,
    In the vanishing of care,
  And of all before and after;
  In the Gods' high banquet, when
    Gleams the grape-flood, flashed to heaven;
  Yea, and in the feasts of men
  Comes his crowned slumber; then
    Pain is dead and hate forgiven!
OTHERS. Loose thy lips from out the rein;
  Lift thy wisdom to disdain;
  Whatso law thou canst not see,
  Scorning; so the end shall be
  Uttermost calamity!
  'Tis the life of quiet breath,
    'Tis the simple and the true,
  Storm nor earthquake shattereth,
    Nor shall aught the house undo
  Where they dwell. For, far away,

---

his other grandson, Actaeon; Pentheus, angry and "tyrannical"; Teiresias speaking like a Christian priest of the Middle Ages, almost like Tennyson's Becket.

[12] The goddess Ὁσία, "Purity," seems to be one of the many abstractions which were half personified by philosophy and by Orphism. It is possible that the word is really adjectival, "Immaculate One," and originally an epithet of some more definite goddess, *e.g.* as Miss Harrison suggests, of Nemesis.

In this and other choruses it is very uncertain how the lines should be distributed between the whole chorus, the two semi-choruses, and the various individual choreutae.

Hidden from the eyes of day,
   Watchers are there in the skies,
   That can see man's life, and prize
Deeds well done by things of clay.
   But the world's Wise are not wise,
Claiming more than mortal may.
Life is such a little thing;
   Lo, their present is departed,
And the dreams to which they cling
Come not. Mad imagining
   Theirs, I ween, and empty-hearted!
DIVERS MAIDENS. Where is the Home for me?
   O Cyprus, set in the sea,
Aphrodite's home In the soft sea-foam,
   Would I could wend to thee;
Where the wings of the Loves are furled,
And faint the heart of the world.

   Aye, unto Paphos' isle,
   Where the rainless meadows smile
With riches rolled From the hundred-fold
   Mouths of the far-off Nile,
Streaming beneath the waves
To the roots of the seaward caves.

   But a better land is there
   Where Olympus cleaves the air,
The high still dell Where the Muses dwell,
   Fairest of all things fair!
O there is Grace, and there is the Heart's Desire,
And peace to adore thee, thou Spirit of Guiding Fire!

* * * * *

   A God of Heaven is he,
   And born in majesty;
Yet hath he mirth In the joy of the Earth,
   And he loveth constantly
Her who brings increase,
The Feeder of Children, Peace.

   No grudge hath he of the great;
   No scorn of the mean estate;
But to all that liveth His wine he giveth,
   Griefless, immaculate;

Only on them that spurn
Joy, may his anger burn.

Love thou the Day and the Night;
Be glad of the Dark and the Light;
And avert thine eyes From the lore of the wise,
That have honour in proud men's sight.
The simple nameless herd of Humanity
Hath deeds and faith that are truth enough for me![13]

[*As the Chorus ceases, a party of the guards return, leading in the midst of them* DIONYSUS, *bound. The* SOLDIER *in command stands forth, as* PENTHEUS, *hearing the tramp of feet, comes out from the Castle.*]

SOLDIER. Our quest is finished, and thy prey, O King,
Caught; for the chase was swift, and this wild thing
Most tame; yet never flinched, nor thought to flee,
But held both hands out unresistingly—
No change, no blanching of the wine-red cheek.
He waited while we came, and bade us wreak
All thy decree; yea, laughed, and made my best
Easy, till I for very shame confessed
And said: "O stranger, not of mine own will
I bind thee, but his bidding to fulfil
Who sent me."
　　　　　　　　And those prisoned Maids withal
Whom thou didst seize and bind within the wall
Of thy great dungeon, they are fled, O King.
Free in the woods, a-dance and glorying
To Bromios. Of their own impulse fell
To earth, men say, fetter and manacle,
And bars slid back untouched of mortal hand
Yea, full of many wonders to thy land
Is this man come… Howbeit, it lies with thee!
PENTHEUS. Ye are mad!—Unhand him. Howso swift he be,
My toils are round him and he shall not fly.

[*The guards loose the arms of* DIONYSUS; PENTHEUS *studies him for a while in silence then speaks jeeringly.* DIONYSUS *remains gentle and unafraid.*]

---

[13] For the meaning of these lines, see Introduction to *Euripides*.

Marry, a fair shape for a woman's eye,
Sir stranger! And thou seek'st no more, I ween!
Long curls, withal! That shows thou ne'er hast been
A wrestler!—down both cheeks so softly tossed
And winsome! And a white skin! It hath cost
Thee pains, to please thy damsels with this white
And red of cheeks that never face the light!

[DIONYSUS *is silent.*]

Speak, sirrah; tell me first thy name and race.
DIONYSUS. No glory is therein, nor yet disgrace.
    Thou hast heard of Tmolus, the bright hill of flowers?
PENTHEUS. Surely, the ridge that winds by Sardis towers.
DIONYSUS. Thence am I; Lydia was my fatherland.
PENTHEUS. And whence these revelations, that thy band
    Spreadeth in Hellas?
DIONYSUS. Their intent and use
    Dionysus oped to me, the Child of Zeus.
PENTHEUS. [*brutally.*] Is there a Zeus there, that can still beget
    Young Gods?
DIONYSUS. Nay, only He whose seal was set
    Here in thy Thebes on Semelê.
PENTHEUS. What way
    Descended he upon thee? In full day
    Or vision of night?
DIONYSUS. Most clear he stood, and scanned
    My soul, and gave his emblems to mine hand.
PENTHEUS. What like be they, these emblems?[14]
DIONYSUS. That may none
    Reveal, nor know, save his Elect alone.
PENTHEUS. And what good bring they to the worshipper?
DIONYSUS. Good beyond price, but not for thee to hear.
PENTHEUS. Thou trickster? Thou wouldst prick me on the more
    To seek them out!
DIONYSUS. His mysteries abhor
    The touch of sin-lovers.
PENTHEUS. And so thine eyes
    Saw this God plain; what guise had he?

---

[14] There were generally associated with mysteries, or special forms of worship, certain relics or sacred implements, without which the rites could not be performed. Cf. Hdt. vii. 153, where Telines of Gela stole the sacred implements or emblems of the nether gods, so that no worship could be performed, and the town was, as it were, excommunicated.

DIONYSUS. What guise
    It liked him. 'Twas not I ordained his shape.
PENTHEUS. Aye, deftly turned again. An idle jape,
    And nothing answered!
DIONYSUS. Wise words being brought
    To blinded eyes will seem as things of naught.
PENTHEUS. And comest thou first to Thebes, to have thy God
    Established?
DIONYSUS. Nay; all Barbary hath trod
    His dance ere this.
PENTHEUS. A low blind folk, I ween,
    Beside our Hellenes!
DIONYSUS. Higher and more keen
    In this thing, though their ways are not thy way.
PENTHEUS. How is thy worship held, by night or day?
DIONYSUS. Most oft by night; 'tis a majestic thing,
    The darkness.
PENTHEUS. Ha! with women worshipping?
    'Tis craft and rottenness!
DIONYSUS. By day no less,
    Whoso will seek may find unholiness—
PENTHEUS. Enough! Thy doom is fixed, for false pretence
    Corrupting Thebes.
DIONYSUS. Not mine; but thine, for dense
    Blindness of heart, and for blaspheming God!
PENTHEUS. A ready knave it is, and brazen-browed,
    This mystery-priest!
DIONYSUS. Come, say what it shall be,
    My doom; what dire thing wilt thou do to me?
PENTHEUS. First, shear that delicate curl that dangles there.

[*He beckons to the soldiers, who approach* DIONYSUS.]

DIONYSUS. I have vowed it to my God; 'tis holy hair.

[*The soldiers cut off the tress.*][15]

PENTHEUS. Next, yield me up thy staff!
DIONYSUS. Raise thine own hand
    To take it. This is Dionysus' wand.

---

[15] The stage directions here are difficult. It is conceivable that none of Pentheus' threats are carried out at all; that the God mysteriously paralyses the hand that is lifted to take his rod without Pentheus himself knowing it. But I think it more likely that the humiliation of Dionysus is made, as far as externals go, complete, and that it is not till later that he begins to show his superhuman powers.

[PENTHEUS *takes the staff.*]

PENTHEUS. Last, I will hold thee prisoned here.
DIONYSUS. My Lord
    God will unloose me, when I speak the word.
PENTHEUS. He may, if e'er again amid his bands
    Of saints he hears thy voice!
DIONYSUS. Even now he stands
    Close here, and sees all that I suffer.
PENTHEUS. What?
    Where is he? For mine eyes discern him not.
DIONYSUS. Where I am! 'Tis thine own impurity
    That veils him from thee.
PENTHEUS. The dog jeers at me!
    At me and Thebes! Bind him!

[*The soldiers begin to bind him.*]

DIONYSUS. I charge ye, bind
    Me not! I having vision and ye blind!
PENTHEUS. And I, with better right, say bind the more!

[*The soldiers obey.*]

DIONYSUS. Thou knowest not what end thou seekest, nor
    What deed thou doest, nor what man thou art!
PENTHEUS. [*mocking.*] Agâvê's son, and on the father's part
    Echîon's, hight Pentheus!
DIONYSUS. So let it be,[16]
    A name fore-written to calamity!
PENTHEUS. Away, and tie him where the steeds are tied;
    Aye, let him lie in the manger!—There abide
    And stare into the darkness!—And this rout
    Of womankind that clusters thee about,
    Thy ministers of worship, are my slaves!
    It may be I will sell them o'er the waves,
    Hither and thither; else they shall be set
    To labour at my distaffs, and forget
    Their timbrel and their songs of dawning day!
DIONYSUS. I go; for that which may not be, I may
    Not suffer! Yet for this thy sin, lo, He
    Whom thou deniest cometh after thee

---

[16] The name Pentheus suggests 'mourner,' from *penthos,* 'mourning.'

For recompense. Yea, in thy wrong to us,
Thou hast cast Him into thy prison-house!

[DIONYSUS, *without his wand, his hair shorn, and his arms tightly
bound, is led off by the guards to his dungeon.* PENTHEUS
returns into the Palace.]

CHORUS.

SOME MAIDENS. Acheloüs' roaming daughter,[17]
  Holy Dircê, virgin water,
  Bathed he not of old in thee,
  The Babe of God, the Mystery?
When from out the fire immortal
  To himself his God did take him,
  To his own flesh, and bespake him:
"Enter now life's second portal,
  Motherless Mystery; lo, I break
  Mine own body for thy sake,
    Thou of the Twofold Door, and seal thee
  Mine, O Bromios,"—thus he spake—
  "And to this thy land reveal thee."
ALL. Still my prayer toward thee quivers,
    Dircê, still to thee I hie me;
  Why, O Blessed among Rivers,
    Wilt thou fly me and deny me?
    By His own joy I vow,
    By the grape upon the bough,
  Thou shalt seek Him in the midnight, thou shalt love Him, even
    now!
OTHER MAIDENS. Dark and of the dark impassioned
  Is this Pentheus' blood; yea, fashioned
  Of the Dragon, and his birth
  From Echîon, child of Earth.
He is no man, but a wonder;
    Did the Earth-Child not beget him,
    As a red Giant, to set him
  Against God, against the Thunder?
He will bind me for his prize,
  Me, the Bride of Dionyse;
    And my priest, my friend, is taken
  Even now, and buried lies;
    In the dark he lies forsaken!

---

[17] Acheloüs was the Father of all Rivers.

ALL. Lo, we race with death, we perish,
    Dionysus, here before thee!
Dost thou mark us not, nor cherish,
    Who implore thee, and adore thee?
    Hither down Olympus' side,
    Come, O Holy One defied,
Be thy golden wand uplifted o'er the tyrant in his pride!
A MAIDEN. Oh, where art thou? In thine own
    Nysa,[18] thou our help alone?
O'er fierce beasts in orient lands
    Doth thy thronging thyrsus wave,
    By the high Corycian Cave,
Or where stern Olympus stands;
In the elm-woods and the oaken,
    There where Orpheus harped of old,
    And the trees awoke and knew him,
    And the wild things gathered to him,
As he sang amid the broken
    Glens his music manifold?
Dionysus loveth thee;
Blessed Land of Piërie,
    He will come to thee with dancing,
Come with joy and mystery;
With the Maenads at his hest
Winding, winding to the West;
    Cross the flood of swiftly glancing
Axios in majesty;
Cross the Lydias, the giver[19]
    Of good gifts and waving green;
Cross that Father-Stream of story,
Through a land of steeds and glory
Rolling, bravest, fairest River
    E'er of mortals seen!
A VOICE WITHIN. Io! Io!
    Awake, ye damsels; hear my cry,
        Calling my Chosen; hearken ye!
A MAIDEN. Who speaketh? Oh, what echoes thus?
ANOTHER. A Voice, a Voice, that calleth us![20]

---

[18] An unknown divine mountain, formed apparently to account for the second part of the name Dionysus.

[19] These are rivers of Thrace which Dionysus must cross in his passage from the East, the Lydias, the Axios, and some other, perhaps the Haliacmon, which is called "the father-stream of story."

THE VOICE. Be of good cheer! Lo, it is I,
    The Child of Zeus and Semelê.
A MAIDEN. O Master, Master, it is Thou!
ANOTHER. O Holy Voice, be with us now!
THE VOICE. Spirit of the Chained Earthquake,
    Hear my word; awake, awake!

[*An Earthquake suddenly shakes the pillars of the Castle.*]

A MAIDEN. Ha! what is coming? Shall the hall
    Of Pentheus racked in ruin fall?
LEADER. Our God is in the house! Ye maids adore Him!
CHORUS. We adore Him all!
THE VOICE. Unveil the Lightning's eye; arouse
    The fire that sleeps, against this house!

[*Fire leaps upon the Tomb of Semelê.*]

A MAIDEN. Ah, saw ye, marked ye there the flame
    From Semelê's enhallowed sod
    Awakened? Yea, the Death that came
    Ablaze from heaven of old, the same
    Hot splendour of the shaft of God?
LEADER. Oh cast ye, cast ye, to the earth! The Lord
    Cometh against this house! Oh, cast ye down,
    Ye trembling damsels; He, our own adored,
    God's Child hath come, and all is overthrown!

[*The Maidens cast themselves upon the ground, their eyes earthward.* DIONYSUS, *alone and unbound, enters from the Castle.*]

DIONYSUS. Ye Damsels of the Morning Hills, why lie ye thus dismayed?[21]
    Ye marked him, then, our Master, and the mighty hand he laid
    On tower and rock, shaking the house of Pentheus?—But arise,
    And cast the trembling from your flesh, and lift untroubled eyes.
LEADER. O Light in Darkness, is it thou? O Priest, is this thy face?
    My heart leaps out to greet thee from the deep of loneliness.

---

[20] Bromios, the God of Many Voices—for, whatever the real derivation, the fifth-century Greeks certainly associated the name with βρέμω, 'to roar'—manifests himself as a voice here and below.

[21] This scene in longer metre always strikes me as a little unlike the style of Euripides, and inferior. It may mark one of the parts left unfinished by the poet, and written in by his son. But it may be that I have not understood it.

DIONYSUS. Fell ye so quick despairing, when beneath the Gate I
    passed?
    Should the gates of Pentheus quell me, or his darkness make me
    fast?
LEADER. Oh, what was left if thou wert gone? What could I but
    despair?
    How hast thou 'scaped the man of sin? Who freed thee from the
    snare?
DIONYSUS. I had no pain nor peril; 'twas mine own hand set me free.
LEADER. Thine arms were gyved!
DIONYSUS. Nay, no gyve, no touch, was laid on me!
    'Twas there I mocked him, in his gyves, and gave him dreams for
    food.
    For when he laid me down, behold, before the stall there stood
    A Bull of Offering. And this King, he bit his lips and straight
    Fell on and bound it, hoof and limb, with gasping wrath and sweat.
    And I sat watching!—Then a Voice; and lo, our Lord was come,
    And the house shook, and a great flame stood o'er his mother's
    tomb.
    And Pentheus hied this way and that, and called his thralls amain
    For water, lest his roof-tree burn; and all toiled, all in vain.
    Then deemed a-sudden I was gone; and left his fire, and sped
    Back to the prison portals, and his lifted sword shone red.
    But there, methinks, the God had wrought—I speak but as I
    guess—
    Some dream-shape in mine image; for he smote at emptiness,
    Stabbed in the air, and strove in wrath, as though 'twere me he
    slew.
    Then 'mid his dreams God smote him yet again! He overthrew
    All that high house. And there in wreck for evermore it lies,
    That the day of this my bondage may be sore in Pentheus' eyes!
    And now his sword is fallen, and he lies outworn and wan
    Who dared to rise against his God in wrath, being but man.
    And I uprose and left him, and in all peace took my path
    Force to my Chosen, recking light of Pentheus and his wrath.
    But soft, methinks a footstep sounds even now within the hall;
    'Tis he; how think ye he will stand, and what words speak withal?
    I will endure him gently, though he come in fury hot.
    For still are the ways of Wisdom, and her temper trembleth not!

    [*Enter* PENTHEUS *in fury.*]

PENTHEUS. It is too much! This Eastern knave hath slipped
    His prison, whom I held but now, hard gripped
    In bondage.—Ha! 'Tis he!—What, sirrah, how

Show'st thou before my portals?

[*He advances furiously upon him.*]

DIONYSUS. And set a quiet carriage to thy rage.
PENTHEUS. How comest thou here? How didst thou break thy cage?
    Speak!
DIONYSUS. Said I not, or didst thou mark not me,
    There was One living that should set me free?
PENTHEUS. Who? Ever wilder are these tales of thine.
DIONYSUS. He who first made for man the clustered vine.
PENTHEUS. I scorn him and his vines.
DIONYSUS. For Dionyse
    'Tis well; for in thy scorn his glory lies.
PENTHEUS. [*to his guard.*] Go swift to all the towers, and bar withal
    Each gate!
DIONYSUS. What, cannot God o'erleap a wall?
PENTHEUS. Oh, wit thou hast, save where thou needest it!
DIONYSUS. Whereso it most imports, there is my wit!—
    Nay, peace! Abide till he who hasteth from
    The mountain side with news for thee, be come.
    We will not fly, but wait on thy command.

[*Enter suddenly and in haste a* MESSENGER *from the Mountain.*]

MESSENGER. Great Pentheus, Lord of all this Theban land,
    I come from high Kithaeron, where the frore
    Snow spangles gleam and cease not evermore...
PENTHEUS. And what of import may thy coming bring?
MESSENGER. I have seen the Wild White Women there, O King,
    Whose fleet limbs darted arrow-like but now
    From Thebes away, and come to tell thee how
    They work strange deeds and passing marvel. Yet
    I first would learn thy pleasure. Shall I set
    My whole tale forth, or veil the stranger part?
    Yea Lord, I fear the swiftness of thy heart,
    Thine edged wrath and more than royal soul.
PENTHEUS. Thy tale shall nothing scathe thee.—Tell the whole.
    It skills not to be wroth with honesty.
    Nay, if thy news of them be dark, 'tis he
    Shall pay it, who bewitched and led them on.
MESSENGER. Our herded kine were moving in the dawn
    Up to the peaks, the greyest, coldest time,
    When the first rays steal earthward, and the rime
    Yields, when I saw three bands of them. The one

Autonoë led, one Ino, one thine own
Mother, Agâvê. There beneath the trees
Sleeping they lay, like wild things flung at ease
In the forest; one half sinking on a bed
Of deep pine greenery; one with careless head
Amid the fallen oak leaves; all most cold
In purity—not as thy tale was told
Of wine-cups and wild music and the chase
For love amid the forest's loneliness.
Then rose the Queen Agâvê suddenly
Amid her band, and gave the God's wild cry,
"Awake, ye Bacchanals! I hear the sound
Of horned kine. Awake ye!"—Then, all round,
Alert, the warm sleep fallen from their eyes,
A marvel of swift ranks I saw them rise,
Dames young and old, and gentle maids unwed
Among them. O'er their shoulders first they shed
Their tresses, and caught up the fallen fold
Of mantles where some clasp had loosened hold,
And girt the dappled fawn-skins in with long
Quick snakes that hissed and writhed with quivering tongue.
And one a young fawn held, and one a wild
Wolf cub, and fed them with white milk, and smiled
In love, young mothers with a mother's breast
And babes at home forgotten! Then they pressed
Wreathed ivy round their brows, and oaken sprays
And flowering bryony. And one would raise
Her wand and smite the rock, and straight a jet
Of quick bright water came. Another set
Her thyrsus in the bosomed earth, and there
Was red wine that the God sent up to her,
A darkling fountain. And if any lips
Sought whiter draughts, with dipping finger-tips
They pressed the sod, and gushing from the ground
Came springs of milk. And reed-wands ivy-crowned
Ran with sweet honey, drop by drop.—O King,
Hadst thou been there, as I, and seen this thing,
With prayer and most high wonder hadst thou gone
To adore this God whom now thou rail'st upon!
   Howbeit, the kine-wardens and shepherds straight
Came to one place, amazed, and held debate;
And one being there who walked the streets and scanned
The ways of speech, took lead of them whose hand
Knew but the slow soil and the solemn hill,
And flattering spoke, and asked: "Is it your will,

Masters, we stay the mother of the King,
Agâvê, from her lawless worshipping,
And win us royal thanks?"—And this seemed good
To all; and through the branching underwood
We hid us, cowering in the leaves. And there
Through the appointed hour they made their prayer
And worship of the Wand, with one accord
Of heart and cry—"Iacchos, Bromios, Lord,
God of God born!"—And all the mountain felt,
And worshipped with them; and the wild things knelt
And ramped and gloried, and the wilderness
Was filled with moving voices and dim stress.

Soon, as it chanced, beside my thicket-close
The Queen herself passed dancing, and I rose
And sprang to seize her. But she turned her face
Upon me: "Ho, my rovers of the chase,
My wild White Hounds, we are hunted! Up, each rod
And follow, follow, for our Lord and God!"
Thereat, for fear they tear us, all we fled
Amazed; and on, with hand unweaponed
They swept toward our herds that browsed the green
Hill grass. Great uddered kine then hadst thou seen
Bellowing in sword-like hands that cleave and tear,
A live steer riven asunder, and the air
Tossed with rent ribs or limbs of cloven tread,
And flesh upon the branches, and a red
Rain from the deep green pines. Yea, bulls of pride,
Horns swift to rage, were fronted and aside
Flung stumbling, by those multitudinous hands
Dragged pitilessly. And swifter were the bands
Of garbed flesh and bone unbound withal
Than on thy royal eyes the lids may fall.

Then on like birds, by their own speed upborne,
They swept toward the plains of waving corn
That lie beside Asopus' banks, and bring
To Thebes the rich fruit of her harvesting.
On Hysiae and Erythrae that lie nursed
Amid Kithaeron's bowering rocks, they burst
Destroying, as a foeman's army comes.
They caught up little children from their homes,
High on their shoulders, babes unheld, that swayed
And laughed and fell not; all a wreck they made;
Yea, bronze and iron did shatter, and in play
Struck hither and thither, yet no wound had they;
Caught fire from out the hearths, yea, carried hot

Flames in their tresses and were scorched not!
The village folk in wrath took spear and sword,
And turned upon the Bacchae. Then, dread Lord,
The wonder was. For spear nor barbed brand
Could scathe nor touch the damsels; but the Wand,
The soft and wreathed wand their white hands sped,
Blasted those men and quelled them, and they fled
Dizzily. Sure some God was in these things!
And the holy women back to those strange springs
Returned, that God had sent them when the day
Dawned, on the upper heights; and washed away
The stain of battle. And those girdling snakes
Hissed out to lap the water-drops from cheeks
And hair and breast.
                        Therefore I counsel thee
O King, receive this Spirit, whoe'er he be,
To Thebes in glory. Greatness manifold
Is all about him; and the tale is told
That this is he who first to man did give
The grief-assuaging vine. Oh, let him live;
For if he die, then Love herself is slain,
And nothing joyous in the world again!
LEADER. Albeit I tremble, and scarce may speak my thought
    To a king's face, yet will I hide it not.
    Dionyse is God, no God more true nor higher!
PENTHEUS. It bursts hard by us, like a smothered fire,
    This frenzy of Bacchic women! All my land
    Is made their mock.—This needs an iron hand!
    Ho, Captain! Quick to the Electran Gate;
    Bid gather all my men-at-arms thereat;
    Call all that spur the charger, all who know[22]
    To wield the orbed targe or bend the bow;
    We march to war—'Fore God, shall women dare
    Such deeds against us? 'Tis too much to bear!
DIONYSUS. Thou mark'st me not, O King, and holdest light
    My solemn words; yet, in thine own despite,
    I warn thee still. Lift thou not up thy spear
    Against a God, but hold thy peace, and fear
    His wrath! He will not brook it, if thou fright
    His Chosen from the hills of their delight.
PENTHEUS. Peace, thou! And if for once thou hast slipped chain,
    Give thanks!—Or shall I knot thine arms again?
DIONYSUS. Better to yield him prayer and sacrifice

---

[22] The typical 'Ercles vein' of the tragic tyrant.

Than kick against the pricks, since Dionyse
Is God, and thou but mortal.
PENTHEUS. That will I!
Yea, sacrifice of women's blood, to cry
His name through all Kithaeron!
DIONYSUS. Ye shall fly,
All, and abase your shields of bronzen rim
Before their wands.
PENTHEUS. There is no way with him,
This stranger that so dogs us! Well or ill
I may entreat him, he must babble still!
DIONYSUS. Wait, good my friend! These crooked matters may
Even yet be straightened.

[PENTHEUS *has started as though to seek his army at the gate.*]

PENTHEUS. Aye, if I obey
Mine own slaves' will; how else?
DIONYSUS. Myself will lead
The damsels hither, without sword or steed.
PENTHEUS. How now?—This is some plot against me!
DIONYSUS. What
Dost fear? Only to save thee do I plot.
PENTHEUS. It is some compact ye have made, whereby
To dance these hills for ever!
DIONYSUS. Verily,
That is my compact, plighted with my Lord!
PENTHEUS. [*turning from him.*] Ho, armourers! Bring forth my shield
and sword!—
And thou, be silent!
DIONYSUS. [*after regarding him fixedly, speaks with resignation.*]
Ah!—Have then thy will!

[*He fixes his eyes upon* PENTHEUS *again, while the armourers
bring out his armour; then speaks in a tone of command.*]

Man, thou wouldst fain behold them on the hill
Praying!
PENTHEUS [*who during the rest of this scene, with a few exceptions,
simply speaks the thoughts that* DIONYSUS. *puts into him, losing
power over his own mind.*]
That would I, though it cost me all
The gold of Thebes!
DIONYSUS. So much? Thou art quick to fall
To such great longing.

PENTHEUS. [*somewhat bewildered at what he has said.*] Aye; 'twould
grieve me much
To see them flown with wine.
DIONYSUS. Yet cravest thou such
A sight as would much grieve thee?
PENTHEUS. Yes; I fain
Would watch, ambushed among the pines.
DIONYSUS. 'Twere vain
To hide. They soon will track thee out.
PENTHEUS. Well said!
'Twere best done openly.
DIONYSUS. Wilt thou be led
By me, and try the venture?
PENTHEUS. Aye, indeed!
Lead on. Why should we tarry?
DIONYSUS. First we need
A rich and trailing robe of fine-linen
To gird thee.
PENTHEUS. Nay; am I a woman, then,[23]
And no man more.
DIONYSUS. Wouldst have them slay thee dead?
No man may see their mysteries.
PENTHEUS. Well said'—
I marked thy subtle temper long ere now.
DIONYSUS. 'Tis Dionyse that prompteth me.
PENTHEUS. And how
Mean'st thou the further plan?
DIONYSUS. First take thy way
Within. I will array thee.
PENTHEUS. What array!
The woman's? Nay, I will not.
DIONYSUS. Doth it change
So soon, all thy desire to see this strange
Adoring?
PENTHEUS. Wait! What garb wilt thou bestow
About me?
DIONYSUS. First a long tress dangling low
Beneath thy shoulders.
PENTHEUS. Aye, and next?
DIONYSUS. The same red

---

[23] The robe and coif were, in the original legend, marks of the Thracian dress
worn by the Thracian followers of Dionysus, and notably by Orpheus. The tradition
became fixed that Pentheus wore such a robe and coif; and to the Greeks of
Euripides' time such a dress seemed to be a woman's. Hence this turn of the story.

Robe, falling to thy feet; and on thine head
A snood.

PENTHEUS. And after? Hast thou aught beyond?

DIONYSUS. Surely; the dappled fawn-skin and the wand.

PENTHEUS. [*after a struggle with himself.*] Enough! I cannot wear a
robe and snood.

DIONYSUS. Wouldst liefer draw the sword and spill men's blood?

PENTHEUS. [*again doubting.*] True, that were evil.—Aye; 'tis best to go
First to some place of watch.

DIONYSUS. Far wiser so,
Than seek by wrath wrath's bitter recompense.

PENTHEUS. What of the city streets? Canst lead me hence
Unseen of any?

DIONYSUS. Lonely and untried
Thy path from hence shall be, and I thy guide!

PENTHEUS. I care for nothing, so these Bacchanals
Triumph not against me!... Forward to my halls
Within!—I will ordain what seemeth best.

DIONYSUS. So be it, O King! 'Tis mine to obey thine hest,
Whate'er it be.

PENTHEUS. [*after hesitating once more and waiting.*] Well, I will go—
perchance
To march and scatter them with serried lance.
Perchance to take thy plan.... I know not yet.[24]

[*Exit* PENTHEUS *into the Castle.*]

DIONYSUS. Damsels, the lion walketh to the net!
He finds his Bacchae now, and sees and dies,
And pays for all his sin!—O Dionyse,
This is thine hour and thou not far away.
Grant us our vengeance!—First, O Master, stay
The course of reason in him, and instil
A foam of madness. Let his seeing will,
Which ne'er had stooped to put thy vesture on,
Be darkened, till the deed is lightly done.
Grant likewise that he find through all his streets
Loud scorn, this man of wrath and bitter threats
That made Thebes tremble, led in woman's guise.
    I go to fold that robe of sacrifice

---

[24] This scene of the 'hypnotising'—if one may use the word—of Pentheus
probably depends much on the action, which, however, I have not ventured to
prescribe. Pentheus seems to struggle against the process all through, to be amazed
at himself for consenting, while constantly finding fresh reasons for doing so.

On Pentheus, that shall deck him to the dark.
His mother's gift!—So shall he learn and mark
God's true Son, Dionyse, in fulness God,
Most fearful, yet to man most soft of mood.

[*Exit* DIONYSUS, *following* PENTHEUS *into Castle.*]

CHORUS.

SOME MAIDENS. Will they ever come to me, ever again,
　　　　The long, long dances,
　　　On through the dark till the dim stars wane?
　　　Shall I feel the dew on my throat, and the stream
　　　Of wind in my hair? Shall our white feet gleam
　　　　In the dim expanses?
　　　Oh, feet of a fawn to the greenwood fled,
　　　　Alone in the grass and the loveliness;
　　　Leap of the hunted, no more in dread,
　　　　Beyond the snares and the deadly press:
　　　Yet a voice still in the distance sounds,
　　　A voice and a fear and a haste of hounds;
　　　O wildly labouring, fiercely fleet,
　　　　Onward yet by river and glen...
　　　Is it joy or terror, ye storm-swift feet?...
　　　　To the dear lone lands untroubled of men,
　　　Where no voice sounds, and amid the shadowy green
　　　The little things of the woodland live unseen.

　　　What else is Wisdom? What of man's endeavour
　　　　Or God's high grace, so lovely and so great?
　　　To stand from fear set free, to breathe and wait;
　　　To hold a hand uplifted over Hate;
　　　And shall not Loveliness be loved for ever?[25]
OTHERS. O Strength of God, slow art thou and still,
　　　　Yet failest never!
　　　On them that worship the Ruthless Will,

---

[25] The refrain of this chorus about the fawn is difficult to interpret. I have practically interpolated the third line ("To stand from fear set free, to breathe and wait"), in order (1) to show the connection of ideas; (2) to make clearer the meaning (as I understand it) of the two Orphic formulae, "What is beautiful is beloved for ever," and "A hand uplifted over the head of Hate." If I am wrong, the refrain is probably a mere cry for revenge, in the tone of the refrain, "Hither for doom and deed," on p. 60. It is one of the many passages where there is a sharp antagonism between the two spirits of the Chorus, first, as furious Bacchanals, and, secondly, as exponents of the idealised Bacchic religion of Euripides, which is so strongly expressed in the rest of this wonderful lyric.

On them that dream, doth His judgment wait.
Dreams of the proud man, making great
    And greater ever,
      Things which are not of God. In wide
        And devious coverts, hunter-wise,
      He coucheth Time's unhasting stride,
        Following, following, him whose eyes
      Look not to Heaven. For all is vain,
      The pulse of the heart, the plot of the brain,
      That striveth beyond the laws that live.
      And is thy Fate so much to give,
      Is it so hard a thing to see,
      That the Spirit of God, whate'er it be,
The Law that abides and changes not, ages long,
The Eternal and Nature-born—these things be strong?

What else is Wisdom? What of man's endeavour
    Or God's high grace so lovely and so great?
    To stand from fear set free, to breathe and wait;
    To hold a hand uplifted over Hate;
And shall not Loveliness be loved for ever?
LEADER. Happy he, on the weary sea
Who hath fled the tempest and won the haven.
    Happy whoso hath risen, free,
Above his striving. For strangely graven
    Is the orb of life, that one and another
    In gold and power may outpass his brother,
    And men in their millions float and flow
And seethe with a million hopes as leaven;
    And they win their Will, or they miss their Will,
    And the hopes are dead or are pined for still,
      But whoe'er can know,
      As the long days go,
That To Live is happy, hath found his Heaven!

[*Re-enter* DIONYSUS, *from the Castle.*]

DIONYSUS. O eye that cravest sights thou must not see,
    O heart athirst for that which slakes not! Thee,
    Pentheus, I call; forth and be seen, in guise
    Of woman, Maenad, saint of Dionyse,
    To spy upon His Chosen and thine own
    Mother!

[Enter PENTHEUS, *clad like a Bacchanal, and strangely excited, a
spirit of Bacchic madness overshadowing him.]*

Thy shape, methinks, is like to one
Of Cadmus' royal maids!
PENTHEUS. Yea; and mine eye
Is bright! Yon sun shines twofold in the sky,
Thebes twofold and the Wall of Seven Gates... .
And is it a Wild Bull this,[26] that walks and waits
Before me? There are horns upon thy brow!
What art thou, man or beast! For surely now
The Bull is on thee!
DIONYSUS. He who erst was wrath,
Goes with us now in gentleness. He hath
Unsealed thine eyes to see what thou shouldst see.
PENTHEUS. Say; stand I not as Ino stands, or she
Who bore me?
DIONYSUS. When I look on thee, it seems
I see their very selves!—But stay; why streams
That lock abroad, not where I laid it, crossed
Under the coif?
PENTHEUS. I did it, as I tossed
My head in dancing, to and fro, and cried
His holy music!
DIONYSUS. *[tending him.]* It shall soon be tied
Aright. 'Tis mine to tend thee... Nay, but stand
With head straight.
PENTHEUS. In the hollow of thine hand
I lay me. Deck me as thou wilt.
DIONYSUS. Thy zone
Is loosened likewise; and the folded gown
Not evenly falling to the feet.
PENTHEUS. 'Tis so,
By the right foot. But here methinks, they flow
In one straight line to the heel.
DIONYSUS. *[while tending him.]* And if thou prove
Their madness true, aye, more than true, what love
And thanks hast thou for me?
PENTHEUS. *[not listening to him.]* In my right hand
Is it, or thus, that I should bear the wand

---

[26] Pentheus, in his Bacchic possession, sees fitfully the mystic shapes of the
God beneath the human disguise. This second-sight, the exaltation of spirit, and the
feeling of supernatural strength come to Pentheus as they came to the two Old Men.
But to them the change came peacefully and for good; to Pentheus it comes by
force, stormily and for evil, because his will was against the God.

To be most like to them?
DIONYSUS. Up let it swing
  In the right hand, timed with the right foot's spring... .
  'Tis well thy heart is changed!
PENTHEUS. [*more wildly.*] What strength is this!
  Kithaeron's steeps and all that in them is—
  How say'st thou?—Could my shoulders lift the whole?
DIONYSUS. Surely thou canst, and if thou wilt! Thy soul,
  Being once so sick, now stands as it should stand.
PENTHEUS. Shall it be bars of iron? Or this bare hand
  And shoulder to the crags, to wrench them down?
DIONYSUS. Wouldst wreck the Nymphs' wild temples, and the brown
  Rocks, where Pan pipes at noonday?
PENTHEUS. Nay; not I!
  Force is not well with women. I will lie
  Hid in the pine-brake.
DIONYSUS. Even as fits a spy
  On holy and fearful things, so shalt thou lie!
PENTHEUS. [*with a laugh.*] They lie there now, methinks—the wild
    birds, caught
  By love among the leaves, and fluttering not!
DIONYSUS. It may be. That is what thou goest to see,
  Aye, and to trap them—so they trap not thee!
PENTHEUS. Forth through the Thebans' town! I am their king,
  Aye, their one Man, seeing I dare this thing!
DIONYSUS. Yea, thou shalt bear their burden, thou alone;
  Therefore thy trial awaiteth thee!—But on;
  With me into thine ambush shalt thou come
  Unscathed; then let another bear thee home!
PENTHEUS. The Queen, my mother.
DIONYSUS. Marked of every eye.
PENTHEUS. For that I go!
DIONYSUS. Thou shalt be borne on high!
PENTHEUS. That were like pride!
DIONYSUS. Thy mother's hands shall share
  Thy carrying.
PENTHEUS. Nay; I need not such soft care!
DIONYSUS. So soft?
PENTHEUS. Whate'er it be, I have earned it well!

[*Exit* PENTHEUS *towards the Mountain.*]

DIONYSUS. Fell, fell art thou; and to a doom so fell
  Thou walkest, that thy name from South to North
  Shall shine, a sign for ever!—Reach thou forth

Thine arms, Agâvê, now, and ye dark-browed
Cadmeian sisters! Greet this prince so proud
To the high ordeal, where save God and me,
None walks unscathed!—The rest this day shall see.

[*Exit* DIONYSUS *following* PENTHEUS.]

CHORUS.

SOME MAIDENS. O hounds raging and blind,[27]
   Up by the mountain road,
  Sprites of the maddened mind,
   To the wild Maids of God;
  Fill with your rage their eyes,
   Rage at the rage unblest,
  Watching in woman's guise,
   The spy upon God's Possessed.
A BACCHANAL. Who shall be first, to mark
   Eyes in the rock that spy,
  Eyes in the pine-tree dark—
   Is it his mother?—and cry:
  "Lo, what is this that comes,
   Haunting, troubling still,
  Even in our heights, our homes,
   The wild Maids of the Hill?
  What flesh bare this child?
   Never on woman's breast
  Changeling so evil smiled;
   Man is he not, but Beast!
  Loin-shape of the wild,
   Gorgon-breed of the waste!"
ALL THE CHORUS. Hither, for doom and deed!
   Hither with lifted sword,
   Justice, Wrath of the Lord,
  Come in our visible need!
  Smite till the throat shall bleed,
  Smite till the heart shall bleed,
  Him the tyrannous, lawless, Godless, Echîon's earthborn seed![28]

---

[27] Spirits of Madness. This lyric prepares us for what follows, especially for Agave's delusion, which other wise might have been hard to understand. I have tried to keep the peculiar metre of the original, the dochmiac, with a few simple licences. The scheme is based on U— —U— or —UU —U—, the latter being much commoner.

[28] The greater part of this chorus is generally abandoned as unintelligible and corrupt. The last ten lines ("Knowledge, we are not foes," &c.) will, I think, make

OTHER MAIDENS. Tyrannously hath he trod;
   Marched him, in Law's despite,
  Against thy Light, O God,
   Yea, and thy Mother's Light;
  Girded him, falsely bold,
   Blinded in craft, to quell
  And by man's violence hold,
  Things unconquerable
A BACCHANAL. A strait pitiless mind
   Is death unto godliness;
  And to feel in human kind
   Life, and a pain the less.
  Knowledge, we are not foes!
   I seek thee diligently;
  But the world with a great wind blows,
   Shining, and not from thee;
  Blowing to beautiful things,
   On, amid dark and light,
  Till Life, through the trammellings
   Of Laws that are not the Right,
  Breaks, clean and pure, and sings
   Glorying to God in the height!
ALL THE CHORUS. Hither for doom and deed!
   Hither with lifted sword,
   Justice, Wrath of the Lord,
  Come in our visible need!
  Smite till the throat shall bleed,
  Smite till the heart shall bleed,
  Him the tyrannous, lawless, Godless, Echîon's earthborn seed!
LEADER. Appear, appear, whatso thy shape or name
   O Mountain Bull, Snake of the Hundred Heads,
     Lion of Burning Flame!
  O God, Beast, Mystery, come! Thy mystic maids
  Are hunted!—Blast their hunter with thy breath,
     Cast o'er his head thy snare;
  And laugh aloud and drag him to his death,
   Who stalks thy herded madness in its lair!

[*Enter hastily a* MESSENGER *from the Mountain, pale and distraught.*]

---

sense if we accept a very slight conjecture of my own, ἀέντων, "let them blow," instead of the impossible ἀεὶ τῶν. The four lines before that ("A strait pitiless mind," &c.) are an almost literal translation of the MS. reading, which, however, is incorrect in metre, and therefore cannot be exactly what Euripides wrote.

MESSENGER. Woe to the house once blest in Hellas! Woe
    To thee, old King Sidonian, who didst sow
    The dragon-seed on Ares' bloody lea!
    Alas, even thy slaves must weep for thee!
LEADER. News from the mountain?—Speak! How hath it sped?
MESSENGER. Pentheus, my king, Echîon's son, is dead!
LEADER. All hail, God of the Voice,
    Manifest ever more!
MESSENGER. What say'st thou?—And how strange thy tone, as though
    In joy at this my master's overthrow!
LEADER. With fierce joy I rejoice,
    Child of a savage shore;
    For the chains of my prison are broken, and the dread where I
        cowered of yore!
MESSENGER. And deem'st thou Thebes so beggared,[29] so forlorn
    Of manhood, as to sit beneath thy scorn?
LEADER. Thebes hath o'er me no sway!
    None save Him I obey,
    Dionysus, Child of the Highest, Him I obey and adore!
MESSENGER. One can forgive thee!—Yet 'tis no fair thing,
    Maids, to rejoice in a man's suffering.
LEADER. Speak of the mountain side!
    Tell us the doom he died,
    The sinner smitten to death, even where his sin was sore!
MESSENGER. We climbed beyond the utmost habitings
    Of Theban shepherds, passed Asopus' springs,
    And struck into the land of rock on dim
    Kithaeron—Pentheus, and, attending him,
    I, and the Stranger who should guide our way,
    Then first in a green dell we stopped, and lay,
    Lips dumb and feet unmoving, warily
    Watching, to be unseen and yet to see.
    A narrow glen it was, by crags o'ertowered,
    Torn through by tossing waters, and there lowered
    A shadow of great pines over it. And there
    The Maenad maidens sate; in toil they were,
    Busily glad. Some with an ivy chain
    Tricked a worn wand to toss its locks again;
    Some, wild in joyance, like young steeds set free,
    Made answering songs of mystic melody.
    But my poor master saw not the great band
    Before him. "Stranger," he cried, "where we stand

---

[29] The couplet is incomplete in the MS. But the sense needed is obvious.

Mine eyes can reach not these false saints of thine.
Mount we the bank, or some high-shouldered pine,
And I shall see their follies clear!" At that
There came a marvel. For the Stranger straight
Touched a great pine-tree's high and heavenward crown,
And lower, lower, lower, urged it down
To the herbless floor. Round like a bending bow,
Or slow wheel's rim a joiner forces to.
So in those hands that tough and mountain stem
Bowed slow—oh, strength not mortal dwelt in them!—
To the very earth. And there he set the King,
And slowly, lest it cast him in its spring.
Let back the young and straining tree, till high
It towered again amid the towering sky;
And Pentheus in the branches! Well, I ween,
He saw the Maenads then, and well was seen!
For scarce was he aloft, when suddenly
There was no stranger any more with me,
But out of Heaven a Voice—oh, what voice else?—
'Twas He that called! "Behold, O damosels,
I bring ye him who turneth to despite
Both me and ye, and darkeneth my great Light.
Tis yours to avenge!" So spake he, and there came
'Twixt earth and sky a pillar of high flame.
And silence took the air, and no leaf stirred
In all the forest dell. Thou hadst not heard
In that vast silence any wild thing's cry.
And up they sprang; but with bewildered eye,
Agaze and listening, scarce yet hearing true.
Then came the Voice again. And when they knew
Their God's clear call, old Cadmus' royal brood,
Up, like wild pigeons startled in a wood,
On flying feet they came, his mother blind,
Agâvê, and her sisters, and behind
All the wild crowd, more deeply maddened then,
Through the angry rocks and torrent-tossing glen,
Until they spied him in the dark pine-tree:
Then climbed a crag hard by and furiously
Some sought to stone him, some their wands would fling
Lance-wise aloft, in cruel targeting.
But none could strike. The height o'ertopped their rage,
And there he clung, unscathed, as in a cage
Caught. And of all their strife no end was found.
Then, "Hither," cried Agâvê; "stand we round
And grip the stem, my Wild Ones, till we take

This climbing cat-o'-the-mount! He shall not make
A tale of God's high dances!" Out then shone
Arm upon arm, past count, and closed upon
The pine, and gripped; and the ground gave, and down
It reeled. And that high sitter from the crown
Of the green pine-top, with a shrieking cry
Fell, as his mind grew clear, and there hard by
Was horror visible. 'Twas his mother stood
O'er him, first priestess of those rites of blood.
He tore the coif, and from his head away
Flung it, that she might know him, and not slay
To her own misery. He touched the wild
Cheek, crying: "Mother, it is I, thy child,
Thy Pentheus, born thee in Echîon's hall!
Have mercy, Mother! Let it not befall
Through sin of mine, that thou shouldst slay thy son!"[30]
    But she, with lips a-foam and eyes that run
Like leaping fire, with thoughts that ne'er should be
On earth, possessed by Bacchios utterly,
Stays not nor hears. Round his left arm she put
Both hands, set hard against his side her foot,
Drew... and the shoulder severed!—not by might
Of arm, but easily, as the God made light
Her hand's essay. And at the other side
Was Ino rending; and the torn flesh cried,
And on Autonoë pressed, and all the crowd
Of ravening arms. Yea, all the air was loud
With groans that faded into sobbing breath,
Dim shrieks, and joy, and triumph-cries of death.
And here was borne a severed arm, and there
A hunter's booted foot; white bones lay bare
With rending; and swift hands ensanguined
Tossed as in sport the flesh of Pentheus dead.
    His body lies afar. The precipice
Hath part, and parts in many an interstice
Lurk of the tangled woodland—no light quest
To find. And, ah, the head! Of all the rest,
His mother hath it, pierced upon a wand,
As one might pierce a lion's, and through the land,
Leaving her sisters in their dancing place,

---

[30] This note of unselfish feeling, of pity and humanity, becomes increasingly marked in all the victims of Dionysus towards the end of the play, and contrasts the more vividly with the God's pitilessness. Cadmus is always gentle, and always thinking of the sufferings of others; and, indeed, so is Agâvê, after her return to reason, though with more resentment against the oppressor.

Bears it on high! Yea, to these walls her face
Was set, exulting in her deed of blood,
Calling upon her Bromios, her God,
Her Comrade, Fellow-Render of the Prey,
Her All-Victorious, to whom this day
She bears in triumph... her own broken heart.
　For me, after that sight, I will depart
Before Agâvê comes.—Oh, to fulfil
God's laws, and have no thought beyond His will,
Is man's best treasure. Aye, and wisdom true,
Methinks, for things of dust to cleave unto!

[*The* MESSENGER *departs into the Castle.*]

CHORUS.

SOME MAIDENS. Weave ye the dance, and call
　　　　Praise to God!
　　Bless ye the Tyrant's fall!
　　　　Down is trod
　　Pentheus, the Dragon's Seed!
　　Wore he the woman's weed?
　　Clasped he his death indeed,
　　　　Clasped the rod?
A BACCHANAL. Yea, the wild ivy lapt him, and the doomed
　　Wild Bull of Sacrifice before him loomed!
OTHERS. Ye who did Bromios scorn,
　　　　Praise Him the more,
　　Bacchanals, Cadmus-born;
　　　　Praise with sore
　　Agony, yea, with tears!
　　Great are the gifts he bears!
　　Hands that a mother rears
　　　　Red with gore!
LEADER. But stay, Agâvê cometh! And her eyes
　　Make fire around her, reeling! Ho, the prize
　　Cometh! All hail, O Rout of Dionyse!

[*Enter from the Mountain* AGÂVÊ, *mad, and to all seeming
wondrously happy, bearing the head of* PENTHEUS *in her
hand. The* CHORUS MAIDENS *stand horror-struck at the sight;
the* LEADER, *also horror-struck, strives to accept it and rejoice
in it as the God's deed.*]

AGÂVÊ. Ye from the lands of Morn!
LEADER. Call me not; I give praise!
AGÂVÊ. Lo, from the trunk new-shorn
　　Hither a Mountain Thorn
　　Bear we! O Asia-born
　　Bacchanals, bless this chase!
LEADER. I see. Yea; I see.
　　Have I not welcomed thee?
AGÂVÊ. [*very calmly and peacefully.*]
　　He was young in the wildwood
　　Without nets I caught him!
　　Nay; look without fear on
　　　The Lion; I have ta'en him!
LEADER. Where in the wildwood?
　　Whence have ye brought him?
AGÂVÊ. Kithaeron...
LEADER. Kithaeron?
AGÂVÊ. The Mountain hath slain him!
LEADER. Who first came nigh him?
AGÂVÊ. I, I, 'tis confessed!
　　And they named me there by him
　　Agâvê the Blessed!
LEADER. Who was next in the band on him?
AGÂVÊ. The daughters....
LEADER. The daughters?
AGÂVÊ. Of Cadmus laid hand on him.
　　But the swift hand that slaughters
　　Is mine; mine is the praise!
　　Bless ye this day of days!

[The LEADER tries to speak, but is not able; AGÂVÊ *begins gently stroking the head.*[31]]

AGÂVÊ. Gather ye now to the feast!
LEADER. Feast!—O miserable!
AGÂVÊ. See, it falls to his breast,
　　Curling and gently tressed,
　　The hair of the Wild Bull's crest—
　　The young steer of the fell!
LEADER. Most like a beast of the wild

[31] It is also possible that by some error of a scribe two lines have been omitted in the MS. But I think the explanation given in the text more probable and more dramatic.

That head, those locks defiled.

AGÂVÊ. [*lifting up the head, more excitedly.*]
He wakened his Mad Ones,
A Chase-God, a wise God!
He sprang them to seize this!
He preys where his band preys.

LEADER. [*brooding, with horror.*] In the trail of thy Mad Ones
Thou tearest thy prize, God!

AGÂVÊ. Dost praise it?

LEADER. I praise this?

AGÂVÊ. Ah, soon shall the land praise!

LEADER. And Pentheus, O Mother,[32]
Thy child?

AGÂVÊ. He shall cry on
My name as none other,
Bless the spoils of the Lion!

LEADER. Aye, strange is thy treasure!

AGÂVÊ. And strange was the taking!

LEADER. Thou art glad?

AGÂVÊ. Beyond measure;
Yea, glad in the breaking
Of dawn upon all this land,
By the prize, the prize of my hand!

LEADER. Show them to all the land, unhappy one,
The trophy of this deed that thou hast done!

AGÂVÊ. Ho, all ye men that round the citadel
And shining towers of ancient Thêbê dwell,
Come! Look upon this prize, this lion's spoil,
That we have taken—yea, with our own toil,
We, Cadmus' daughters! Not with leathern-set
Thessalian javelins, not with hunter's net,
Only white arms and swift hands' bladed fall
Why make ye much ado, and boast withal
Your armourers' engines? See, these palms were bare
That caught the angry beast, and held, and tare[33]
The limbs of him!... Father!... Go, bring to me
My father!... Aye, and Pentheus, where is he,

---

[32] The Leader mentions Pentheus, I suppose, in order deliberately to test Agâvê's delusion, to see if she is indeed utterly unconscious of the truth.

[33] This marvellous scene defies comment. But I may be excused for remarking (1) that the psychological change of the chorus is, to my mind, proved by the words of the original, and does not in the least depend on my interpolated stage directions; (2) the extraordinary exultation of Agâvê is part of her Bacchic possession. It is not to be supposed that, if she had really killed a lion, such joy would be the natural thing.

My son? He shall set up a ladder-stair
Against this house, and in the triglyphs there
Nail me this lion's head, that gloriously
I bring ye, having slain him—I, even I!

[*She goes through the crowd towards the Castle, showing the head
and looking for a place to hang it. Enter from the Mountain*
CADMUS, *with attendants, bearing the body of* PENTHEUS *on a
bier.*]

CADMUS. On, with your awful burden. Follow me,
    Thralls, to his house, whose body grievously
    With many a weary search at last in dim
    Kithaeron's glens I found, torn limb from limb,
    And through the intervening forest weed
    Scattered.—Men told me of my daughters' deed,
    When I was just returned within these walls,
    With grey Teiresias, from the Bacchanals.
    And back I hied me to the hills again
    To seek my murdered son. There saw I plain
    Actaeon's mother, ranging where he died,
    Autonoë; and Ino by her side,
    Wandering ghastly in the pine-copses.
        Agâvê was not there. The rumour is
    She cometh fleet-foot hither.—Ah! 'Tis true;
    A sight I scarce can bend mine eyes unto.
AGÂVÊ. [*turning from the Palace and seeing him.*] My father, a great
    boast is thine this hour.
    Thou hast begotten daughters, high in power
    And valiant above all mankind—yea, all
    Valiant, though none like me! I have let fall
    The shuttle by the loom, and raised my hand
    For higher things, to slay from out thy land
    Wild beasts! See, in mine arms I bear the prize,
    That nailed above these portals it may rise
    To show what things thy daughters did! Do thou
    Take it, and call a feast. Proud art thou now
    And highly favoured in our valiancy!
CADMUS. O depth of grief, how can I fathom thee
    Or look upon thee!—Poor, poor bloodstained hand!
    Poor sisters!—A fair sacrifice to stand
    Before God's altars, daughter; yea, and call
    Me and my citizens to feast withal!
        Nay, let me weep—for thine affliction most,
    Then for mine own. All, all of us are lost,

Not wrongfully, yet is it hard, from one
Who might have loved—our Bromios, our own!

AGÂVÊ. How crabbed and how scowling in the eyes
Is man's old age!—Would that my son likewise
Were happy of his hunting, in my way
When with his warrior bands he will essay
The wild beast!—Nay, his valiance is to fight
With God's will! Father, thou shouldst set him right.
Will no one bring him thither, that mine eyes
May look on his, and show him this my prize!

CADMUS. Alas, if ever ye can know again
The truth of what ye did, what pain of pain
That truth shall bring! Or were it best to wait
Darkened for evermore, and deem your state
Not misery, though ye know no happiness?

AGÂVÊ. What seest thou here to chide, or not to bless?

CADMUS. [*after hesitation, resolving himself.*] Raise me thine eyes to
yon blue dome of air!

AGÂVÊ. 'Tis done. What dost thou bid me seek for there?

CADMUS. Is it the same, or changed in thy sight?

AGÂVÊ. More shining than before, more heavenly bright![34]

CADMUS. And that wild tremour, is it with thee still?

AGÂVÊ. [*troubled.*] I know not what thou sayest; but my will
Clears, and some change cometh, I know not how.

CADMUS. Canst hearken then, being changed, and answer, now!

AGÂVÊ. I have forgotten something; else I could.

CADMUS. What husband led thee of old from mine abode?

AGÂVÊ. Echîon, whom men named the Child of Earth.

CADMUS. And what child in Echîon's house had birth?

AGÂVÊ. Pentheus, of my love and his father's bred.

CADMUS. Thou bearest in thine arms an head—what head?

AGÂVÊ. [*beginning to tremble, and not looking at what she carries.*] A
lion's—so they all said in the chase.

CADMUS. Turn to it now—'tis no long toil—and gaze.

AGÂVÊ. Ah! But what is it? What am I carrying here?

CADMUS. Look once upon it full, till all be clear!

AGÂVÊ. I see... most deadly pain! Oh, woe is me!

CADMUS. Wears it the likeness of a lion to thee?

AGÂVÊ. No; 'tis the head—O God!—of Pentheus, this!

CADMUS. Blood-drenched ere thou wouldst know him! Aye, 'tis his.

AGÂVÊ. Who slew him?—How came I to hold this thing?

---

[34] The sight of the pure heaven brings back light to her mind—that is clear.
But does she mean that the sky is brighter because of her madness which still
remains, or that it is brighter now, after having been darkened in her madness?

CADMUS. O cruel Truth, is this thine home-coming?

AGÂVÊ. Answer! My heart is hanging on thy breath!

CADMUS. 'Twas thou.—Thou and thy sisters wrought his death.

AGÂVÊ. In what place was it? His own house, or where?

CADMUS. Where the dogs tore Actaeon, even there.

AGÂVÊ. Why went he to Kithaeron? What sought he?

CADMUS. To mock the God and thine own ecstasy.

AGÂVÊ. But how should we be on the hills this day?

CADMUS. Being mad! A spirit drove all the land that way.

AGÂVÊ. 'Tis Dionyse hath done it! Now I see.

CADMUS. [*earnestly.*] Ye wronged Him! Ye denied his deity!

AGÂVÊ. [*turning from him.*] Show me the body of the son I love!

CADMUS. [*leading her to the bier.*] 'Tis here, my child. Hard was the quest thereof.

AGÂVÊ. Laid in due state?

[*As there is no answer, she lifts the veil of the bier, and sees.*]

Oh, if I wrought a sin,
'Twas mine! What portion had my child therein!

CADMUS. He made him like to you, adoring not
The God; who therefore to one bane hath brought
You and this body, wrecking all our line,
And me. Aye, no man-child was ever mine;
And now this first-fruit of the flesh of thee,
Sad woman, foully here and frightfully
Lies murdered! Whom the house looked up unto,

[*Kneeling by the body.*]

O Child, my daughter's child! who heldest true
My castle walls; and to the folk a name
Of fear thou wast; and no man sought to shame
My grey beard, when they knew that thou wast there,
Else had they swift reward!—And now I fare
Forth in dishonour,[35] outcast, I, the great
Cadmus, who sowed the seed-rows of this state
Of Thebes, and reaped the harvest wonderful.
O my beloved, though thy heart is dull
In death, O still beloved, and alway
Beloved! Never more, then, shalt thou lay

---

[35] He has not yet been sentenced to exile, though he might well judge that after such pollution all his family would be banished. But probably this is another mark of the unrevised state of the play.

Thine hand to this white beard, and speak to me
Thy "Mother's Father"; ask "Who wrongeth thee?
Who stints thine honour, or with malice stirs
Thine heart? Speak, and I smite thine injurers!"
But now—woe, woe, to me and thee also,
Woe to thy mother and her sisters, woe
Alway! Oh, whoso walketh not in dread
Of Gods, let him but look on this man dead!

LEADER. Lo, I weep with thee. 'Twas but due reward
  God sent on Pentheus; but for thee... 'Tis hard.
AGÂVÊ. My father, thou canst see the change in me,

* * * * *
* * * * *

[*A page or more has here been torn out of the MS. from which all
our copies of "The Bacchae" are derived. It evidently
contained a speech of* AGÂVÊ *[followed presumably by some
words of the Chorus.], and an appearance of* DIONYSUS *upon
a cloud. He must have pronounced judgment upon the
Thebans in general, and especially upon the daughters of*
CADMUS, *have justified his own action, and declared his
determination to establish his godhead. Where the MS begins
again, we find him addressing* CADMUS.]

* * * * *

DIONYSUS. And tell of Time, what gifts for thee he bears,
  What griefs and wonders in the winding years.
  For thou must change and be a Serpent Thing
  Strange, and beside thee she whom thou didst bring[36]

---

[36] A prophecy like this is a very common occurrence in the last scenes of
Euripides' tragedies. "The subject of the play is really a long chain of events. The
poet fixes on some portion of it—the action of one day, generally speaking—and
treats it as a piece of vivid concrete life, led up to by a merely narrative introduction
(the Prologue), and melting away into a merely narrative close. The method is to
our taste undramatic, but it is explicable enough. It falls in with the tendency of
Greek art to finish, not with a climax, but with a lessening of strain" (*Greek
Literature*, p. 267).

The prophecy was that Cadmus and Harmonia should be changed into
serpents and should lead a host of barbarian invaders—identified with an Illyrian
tribe, the Encheleis—against Hellas; they should prosper until they laid hands on
the treasures of Delphi, and then be destroyed. Herodotus says that the Persians
were influenced by this prophecy when they refrained from attacking Delphi (Hdt.
ix. 42).

Of old to be thy bride from Heaven afar,
Harmonia, daughter of the Lord of War.
Yea, and a chariot of kine—so spake
The word of Zeus—thee and thy Queen shall take
Through many lands, Lord of a wild array
Of orient spears. And many towns shall they
Destroy beneath thee, that vast horde, until
They touch Apollo's dwelling, and fulfil
Their doom, back driven on stormy ways and steep.
Thee only and thy spouse shall Ares keep,
And save alive to the Islands of the Blest.
   Thus speaketh Dionysus, Son confessed
Of no man but of Zeus!—Ah, had ye seen
Truth in the hour ye would not, all had been
Well with ye, and the Child of God your friend!

AGÂVÊ. Dionysus, we beseech thee! We have sinned!

DIONYSUS. Too late! When there was time, ye knew me not!

AGÂVÊ. We have confessed. Yet is thine hand too hot.

DIONYSUS. Ye mocked me, being God; this your wage.

AGÂVÊ. Should God be like a proud man in his rage?

DIONYSUS. 'Tis as my sire, Zeus, willed it long ago.

AGÂVÊ. [*turning from him almost with disdain.*] Old man, the word is
   spoken; we must go.

DIONYSUS. And seeing ye must, what is it that ye wait?

CADMUS. Child, we are come into a deadly strait,
   All; thou, poor sufferer, and thy sisters twain,
   And my sad self. Far off to barbarous men,
   A grey-haired wanderer, I must take my road.
   And then the oracle, the doom of God,
   That I must lead a raging horde far-flown
   To prey on Hellas; lead my spouse, mine own
   Harmonia. Ares' child, discorporate
   And haunting forms, dragon and dragon-mate,
   Against the tombs and altar-stones of Greece,
   Lance upon lance behind us; and not cease
   From toils, like other men, nor dream, nor past
   The foam of Acheron find my peace at last.

AGÂVÊ. Father! And I must wander far from thee!

CADMUS. O Child, why wilt thou reach thine arms to me,
   As yearns the milk-white swan, when old swans die?

AGÂVÊ. Where shall I turn me else? No home have I.

CADMUS. I know not; I can help thee not.

AGÂVÊ. Farewell, O home, O ancient tower!
   Lo, I am outcast from my bower,
   And leave ye for a worser lot.

CADMUS. Go forth, go forth to misery,
The way Actaeon's father went!
AGÂVÊ. Father, for thee my tears are spent.
CADMUS. Nay, Child, 'tis I must weep for thee;
For thee and for thy sisters twain!
AGÂVÊ. On all this house, in bitter wise,
Our Lord and Master, Dionyse,
Hath poured the utter dregs of pain!
DIONYSUS. In bitter wise, for bitter was the shame
Ye did me, when Thebes honoured not my name.
AGÂVÊ. Then lead me where my sisters be;
Together let our tears be shed,
Our ways be wandered; where no red
Kithaeron waits to gaze on me;

Nor I gaze back; no thyrsus stem,
Nor song, nor memory in the air.
Oh, other Bacchanals be there,
Not I, not I, to dream of them!

[AGÂVÊ *with her group of attendants goes out on the side away from the Mountain.* DIONYSUS *rises upon the Cloud and disappears.*]

CHORUS. There may be many shapes of mystery,
And many things God makes to be,
Past hope or fear.
And the end men looked for cometh not,
And a path is there where no man thought.
So hath it fallen here. [*Exeunt.*]

THE END

Made in the USA
Las Vegas, NV
16 February 2021

17951422R00032